# SECURE AND RECOGNIZED BOUNDARIES

ISRAEL'S RIGHT TO LIVE IN PEACE
WITHIN DEFENSIBLE FRONTIERS

ELEMENTS
IN THE CONSIDERATION OF ISRAEL'S POSITION
ON THE QUESTION OF BOUNDARIES

Carta, Jerusalem

Prepared by Carta, Jerusalem
Plates by E. Pikovsky Ltd., Jerusalem
Printed at The Jerusalem Post Press, Jerusalem

# CONTENTS

".. . their right to live in **peace** within **secure** and **recognized** boundaries **free** from threats or acts of force .. ."

*United Nations Security Council Resolution 242— November 1967*


".. . borders that are defensible .. ."

*President Richard M. Nixon: 1 July 1970*


"Historically there have never been secure or recognized boundaries of the area. Neither the armistice lines of 1949, nor the cease-fire lines of 1967 have answered that description . . . such boundaries have yet to be agreed upon . . . an agreement on that point is an absolute essential to a just and lasting peace . . . history shows that imposed boundaries are not secure and that secure boundaries must be mutually worked out and recognized by the parties themselves as part of the peace-making process."

*United States Ambassador Arthur Goldberg in the United Nations Security Council—15 November 1967*

# 1973
# CEASE – FIRE

*Mediterranean*

*Sea*

Beirut

LEBANON

Damascus

Tyre

Akko  Safad
Haifa      Kuneitra
        Tiberias    SYRIA

Beit-Shean
Hadera
Netanya

Nablus

Tel-Aviv-
Jaffa

Ashdod

Amman

Jerusalem

Gaza

Hebron

JORDAN

Beer Sheba

Kerak

El Arish

Abu Aweigila

Kusseima

Bir Gafgafa

Port Sa'id

Kantara

Suez

Ma'an

SINAI

Eilat

Mudawwara

Abu Rudeis

SAUDI ARABIA

Dahab

EGYPT

Tur

Nabek
Tiran
Sanafir
Sharm e-Sheikh
*Red Sea*

0    25    50
km
CARTA, Jerusalem

This booklet, first published in 1971, explains Israel's need for secure and recognized boundaries. The Yom Kippur War has once again

3

shown the importance of the territorial dimension. Because of her defensive depth this was the first Arab-Israeli war fought at a distance from Israel's population centres.

Had the same sophisticated Soviet weaponry which the Arabs threw initially into the war been used against Israel in its pre-1967 borders, they would surely have cut off the southern Negev from the rest of the country, cast the vulnerable northern "finger" of the Galilee into Syrian hands and cost Israel many more casualties.

It is, therefore, natural for Israel to view the territorial issue as the major subject in peace negotiations.

The fact that the war was carefully planned gave the attackers an initial advantage which gained them a measure of penetration into both Sinai and the Golan Heights. However, Israel's strategic depth permitted the I.D.F. to contain the attack and launch a counter-attack on both fronts: Israel Defense Forces thrust into Syria, holding ground some 40 kilometres from Damascus. In Sinai the I.D.F. forced a crossing of the Suez Canal and surrounded the town of Suez, commanding key transport lines from the Egyptian heartland to the southern part of the Canal. (See map)

# INTRODUCTION

There is a radical difference between Israel's border problems and those many other cases of boundary litigation and frontier differences to which the world has been accustomed (from time immemorial). Invariably, these are conflicts between sovereign States over segments of territory, rivers or strategic areas, which they claim from each other, citing historic precedent or previous awards or arrangements.

The special feature affecting the border between Israel and the Arab States is that the latter not only still contend that a state of war exists between them and Israel, but that they actually contest Israel's very existence as a State. Thus, in effect, they oppose any final delimitation of Israel's borders. They continue to do so in spite of the fact that Israel's re-establishment in its ancient Homeland has been expressly endorsed and supported by the family of nations; also that both the Arab States and Israel are members of the United Nations, whose Charter specifically enjoins members to recognize and live in peace with each other.

The Arab-Israeli conflict is actually the story of the continued warfare and belligerency of the Arab States against Israel. This conflict has never centred on the delineation of borders or indeed the disposition of territory. It has centred on the basic Arab desire to eliminate Israel altogether, (a desire which has been frustrated by Israel's resolute self-defence).

Following the Six-Day War, unleashed by the Arabs in 1967 in a sudden resurgence of active belligerency and blockade, the United Nations Security Council, on 22 November 1967, called for the establishment of a "just and lasting peace" between the Arab States and Israel that would give Israel and the Arab States the "right to live within secure and recognized boundaries."

The Council, and before it the General Assembly, rejected all attempts and proposals sponsored by the Arabs and their supporters to bring about an unrequited Israeli withdrawal without the conclusion of final and permanent peace treaties. Such an unrequited withdrawal, accompanied by vague international guarantees and the stationing of United Nations observer units, had been carried out after an earlier upsurge of Arab hostility, in 1956–7. Its essential unreality was demonstrated in 1967 when the Arab States, with the active backing of the Soviet Union, decided that the moment had arrived to attempt the destruction of Israel once again.

The Security Council called for "secure and recognized boundaries" because such, or indeed any boundaries at all, had never before existed between Israel and the Arab States. Israel, in its modern regeneration, has known only fragile armistice and temporary demarcation lines, truce arrangements or cease-fire lines, always reflecting the military situation at the end of the periods of fighting initiated by Arab attacks. The temporary nature of the 1949 armistice lines, for instance was stressed in each of the separate armistice agreements signed between Israel and the Arab States at the end of the Arab invasion of nascent Israel, and Arab representatives were always vociferous in insisting on their temporary and exclusively military nature. Syria refused to accept the Security Council's November 1967 Resolution.

Israel's history in the Middle East goes back to the dawn of recorded history. It is the only country in the region whose people live in the same area, speak the same language and maintain traditions and memories of three thousand years ago. It is only under Jewish rule and Jewish sovereignty that the area in question maintained its uniqueness or, indeed, its own geographic entity. It was conquered and reconquered no less than fourteen times in thirty centuries, yet no conquest—with the brief and solitary exception of the Crusades—resulted in more than administration from without.

Throughout this period and even in spite of enforced dispersion the Jewish community maintained its presence in the Land while Jews dispersed abroad kept an unbroken link with their Homeland throughout the generations, praying for its redemption and celebrating its seasons and remembering its map and geographic features. The Land as an entity thus goes back to biblical times.

The following pages and the accompanying maps trace the history and dimensions of the Land's borders through the centuries. They throw light on the current discussions about the "secure and recognized" borders sought by modern Israel in conformity with the Security Council Resolution.

A concluding section devoted to boundary changes in Europe supplies the background of general international practice in such matters.

6

# HISTORY

# 10th–6th Century BCE
# THE PERIOD OF THE FIRST TEMPLE

★   During the second half of the millennium BCE, Israeli tribes became established in the territories on both sides of the River Jordan.

★   During the Tenth Century BCE tribal organization became consolidated into a kingdom.

★   The map on the opposite page shows the boundaries of the kingdom in the days of David and Solomon, its founders.

It was later divided into two: the southern kingdom of Judah and the northern kingdom of Israel.

★   In 734 BCE the kingdom of Israel was conquered by the Assyrians, who destroyed its political unity and divided it into several provinces.

★   In 587 BCE the kingdom of Judah was finally conquered by the Babylonians and the First Temple was destroyed. A large part of the population was carried off to Babylon.

8

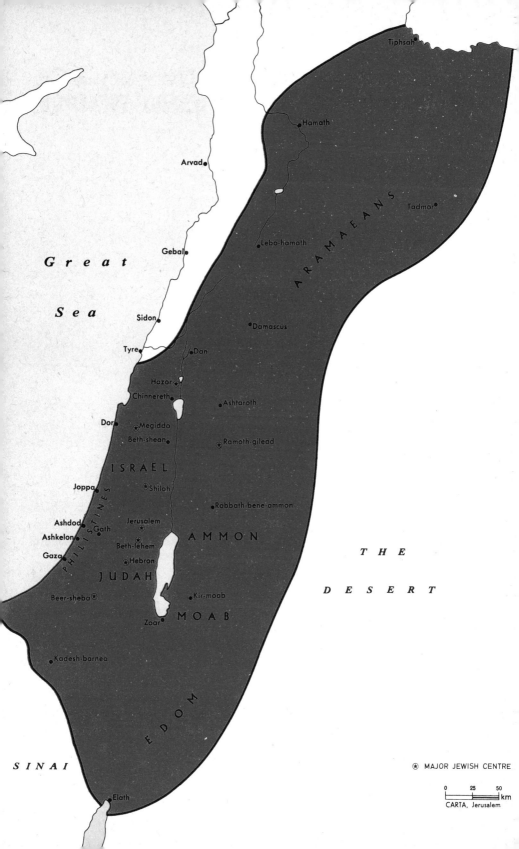

Great

Sea

SINAI

Tiphsah

Hamath

Arvad

Tadmor

Gebal

Lebo-hamath

A R A M A E A N S

Sidon

Damascus

Tyre

Dan

Hazor

Chinnereth

Ashtaroth

Dor

Megiddo

Beth-shean

Ramoth-gilead

I S R A E L

Joppa

Shiloh

Rabbath-bene-ammon

Ashdod

Gath

Jerusalem

Ashkelon

A M M O N

T H E

Gaza

Beth-lehem

Hebron

D E S E R T

J U D A H

Beer-sheba

Kir-moab

Zoar

M O A B

Kadesh-barnea

E D O M

⊛ MAJOR JEWISH CENTRE

0   25   50
km
CARTA, Jerusalem

Elath

# 6th Century BCE–1st Century BCE
# THE PERIOD OF SECOND TEMPLE

★ The Jewish exiles in Babylon retained their identity, and in 536 BCE Cyrus of Persia (then the dominant Empire) permitted them to return to their land and to rebuild the Temple, and granted them a measure of autonomy.

★ During the succeeding centuries, their culture developed and with it their independence grew, asserting itself completely when the Maccabees revolted in 167 BCE against Hellenistic suzerainty.

★ Alexander Yanai, King and High Priest of the Jews (103–76 BCE) established Jewish sovereignty throughout most of the Land from the sea to the desert. Subsequently, King Herod (37–4 BCE) consolidated the kingdom. The map opposite shows the extent of his territories.

★ Jewish independence collapsed in 70 CE after a long war of resistance against the Romans. The Second Temple was destroyed. A later revolt against the Romans, led by Bar Kochba, was suppressed in 135 CE.

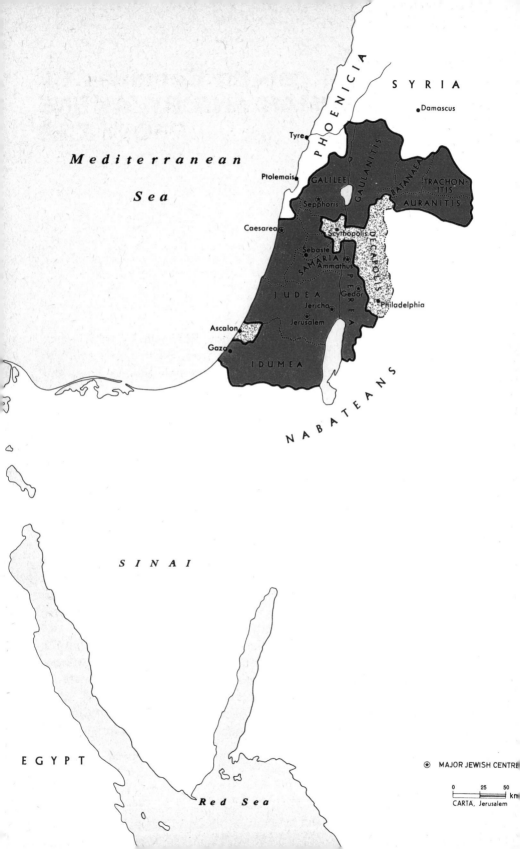

S Y R I A

•Damascus

Mediterranean

Sea

Tyre•

P H O E N I C I A

Ptolemais•

GALILEE

GAULANITIS

BATANAEA

TRACHON-
ITIS

Caesarea•

Sepphoris•

AURANITIS

Scythopolis□

DECAPOLIS

Sebaste•

SAMARIA

Ammathus•

Gedor•

PEREA

Philadelphia•

JUDEA

Jericho•

Ascalon•

Jerusalem•

Gaza•

I D U M E A

N A B A T E A N S

S I N A I

E G Y P T

Red Sea

⊛  MAJOR JEWISH CENTRE

0        25      50
⊢━━━┴━━━┤  km
CARTA, Jerusalem

# 1st–7th Centuries CE
# ROMAN AND BYZANTINE
# PROVINCES

★ The Romans first renamed the Land "Provincia Judaea", which encompassed much of its previous area from Sinai in the south to Galilee in the north and from the Mediterranean Sea to deep into present-day Jordan, across the Jordan river.

★ The Jews persistently endeavoured to throw off the yoke of the conqueror. This was met by the Romans by brutal repression and measures of expulsion and by an attempt to change historic names to prevent the ancient nomenclature from serving as a focus of the Jewish people's hopes and aspirations.

★ Thus the Romans renamed Jerusalem "Aelia Capitolina", while "Provincia Judaea" was changed to "Provincia Syria–Palaestina". The name "Palaestina" was derived from the ancient Philistines who had occupied a small part of the coastal plain, while the name Syria was added in order to stifle any local separatism. Subsequently "Syria" was discarded and the name "Provincia Palaestina" was left.

★ That episode, too, was short-lived, and soon the Romans resorted to the familiar pattern employed by conquerors, the division of the Land into smaller, independently administered parts.

★ By 356 CE "Palaestina" was split into two provinces and in 425 into three: Palaestina Prima, Palaestina Secunda and Palaestina Tertia. Taken together, the boundaries of the three provinces, as shown on the opposite page, once again roughly encompass the Land in its historic dimensions, including the present-day Golan Heights, Judaea and Samaria and a slice of Sinai, and a major part of present-day Jordan, east of the river.

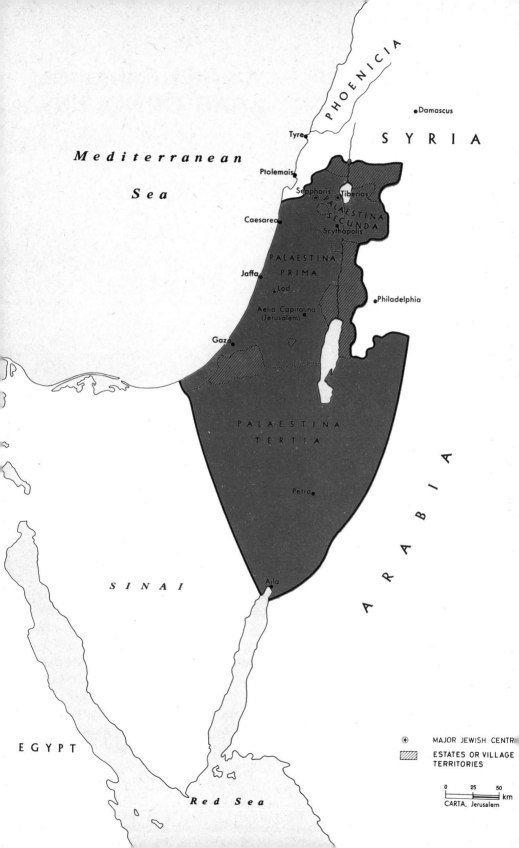

PHOENICIA

SYRIA

•Damascus

Mediterranean

Sea

Tyre•

Ptolemais•

Sephoris•  ✴Tiberias

PALAESTINA
SECUNDA

Caesarea•

Scythopolis•

PALAESTINA
PRIMA

Jaffa•

•Lod

•Philadelphia

Aelia Capitolina
(Jerusalem)•

Gaza•

PALAESTINA
TERTIA

SINAI

Petra•

A R A B I A

Aila•

EGYPT

Red Sea

✴   MAJOR JEWISH CENTRE

▨   ESTATES OR VILLAGE
    TERRITORIES

0      25      50
▬▬▬▬▬▬▬▬ km
CARTA, Jerusalem

# 7th–11th Centuries
# ARAB CONQUEST

★   After the Arab conquest, Palaestina Prima was turned into the Jund (military district) of Falastin which again derives from the Philistines. Its capital was removed from Jerusalem, which had been allowed to become derelict, to the district hamlet of Ramla, half-way between present-day Tel Aviv and the capital city of Jerusalem. Ramla is the only town founded by the Arabs in the whole history of the Land.

★   Palaestina Secunda was renamed the Jund Urdun (Jordan military district). It consisted of part of Galilee, with the country further to the north forming part of the Damascus district, the capital of the invading forces.

With the dissolution of the Abbasid Empire, all semblance of centralized control disappeared. The Land fell into the hands of local chieftains. Anarchy brought further destruction and desolation. Yet, throughout, a Jewish community clung to the Land, hoping, praying and working for the re-establishment of the ancestral Homeland.

★   The map shows the areas of the Arab military occupation districts.

14

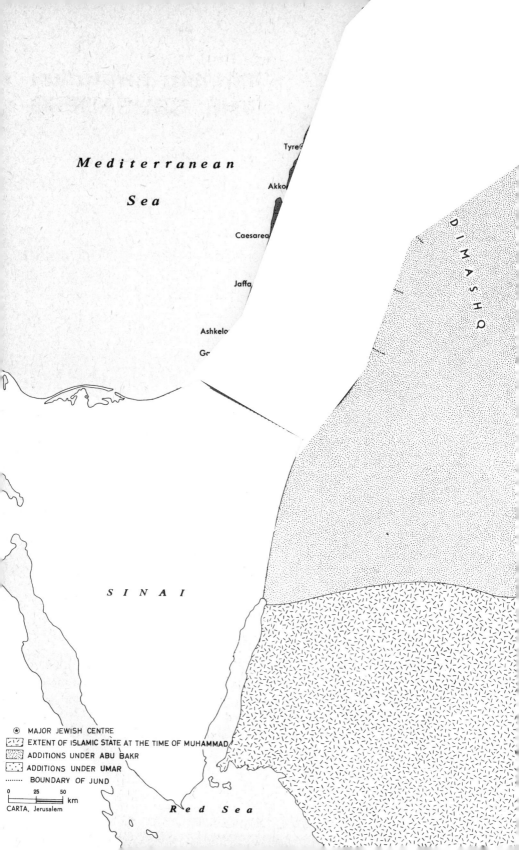

*Mediterranean*

*Sea*

Tyre

Akko

Caesarea

Jaffa

Ashkelo

G

D I M A S H Q

*S I N A I*

⊛ MAJOR JEWISH CENTRE
EXTENT OF ISLAMIC STATE AT THE TIME OF MUHAMMAD
ADDITIONS UNDER ABU BAKR
ADDITIONS UNDER UMAR
·········· BOUNDARY OF JUND

0    25    50
km

CARTA, Jerusalem

*R e d   S e a*

# 11th-13th Centuries
# THE CRUSADERS

★   The Crusaders established a kingdom in the Land from 1099 to 1176, when they were defeated by Saladin. One of the principal factors in their failure was that they were never more than a small and alien ruling class, without roots in the land.

★   The map shows the Crusader Kingdom of Jerusalem in the 12th Century.

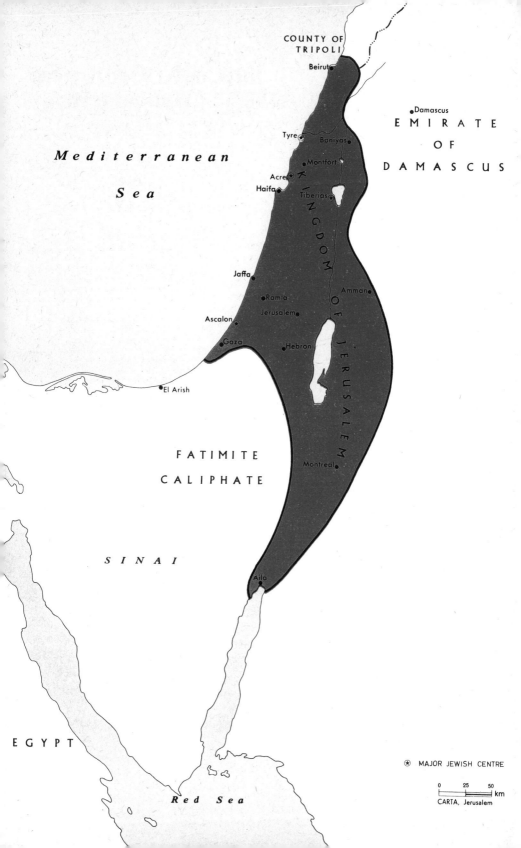

COUNTY OF
TRIPOLI

•Beirut

Mediterranean

Sea

•Damascus

E M I R A T E

O F

D A M A S C U S

Tyre
Baniyas

•Montfort

Acre⊛
Haifa

Tiberias

K
I
N
G
D
O
M

O
F

J
E
R
U
S
A
L
E
M

•Jaffa

•Amman

•Ramla

•Jerusalem

Ascalon•

•Hebron

•Gaza

•El Arish

F A T I M I T E

C A L I P H A T E

•Montreal

S I N A I

•Aila

E G Y P T

Red Sea

⊛  MAJOR JEWISH CENTRE

0      25      50
|⊢——⊢——⊣| km
CARTA, Jerusalem

# 13th-20th Centuries
# MAMLUK AND OTTOMAN RULE

★   After the disappearance of the Crusaders the Land became a province of the Mamluk kingdom, until the beginning of the 16th century.

★   For four centuries, from 1517 until 1918, the Land was a province of the Ottoman Empire.

★   The accompanying map shows the administrative districts of the Ottoman Empire, with the regional headquarters, again including the Jewish communities in cities such as Jerusalem and Hebron, Safad and Tiberias.

★   Of particular interest is the delimitation of the boundary in Sinai. Prior to 1906 the frontier had run along a line from Suez to El Arish. Following the construction of the Canal, the British, who were then in control of Egypt, wished to push the Turks as far as possible to the north and the east.

With Turkey's increasing political closeness to the Central Powers, primarily Germany, Britain's imperial interests called for an extended territorial buffer. It therefore took advantage of Turkey's military weakness to move the boundary to between Rafah and Taba, where it stood from 1906 until 1949.

★   The map shows the various Ottoman provinces as well as the shifting border.

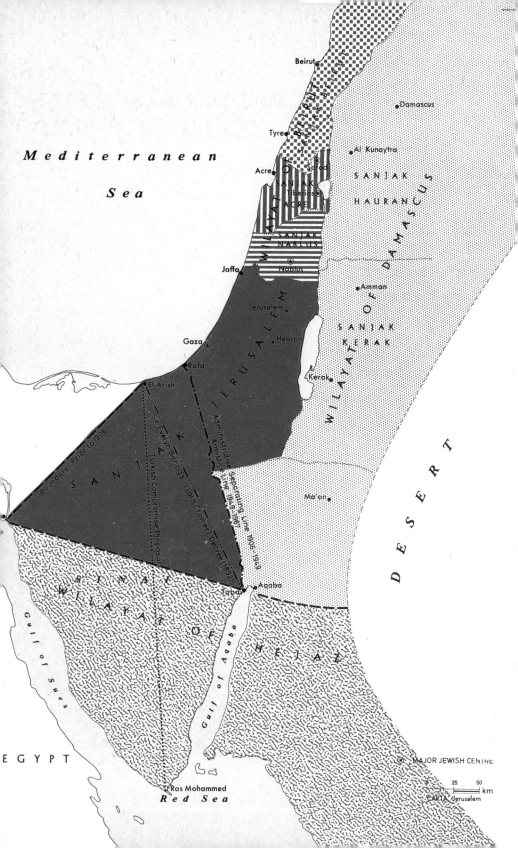

Beirut

Damascus

*SANJAK OF BEIRUT*

Tyre

Al Kunaytra

Acre
Safad

*SANJAK*

Tiberias

*HAURAN*

*SANJAK*
*ACRE*

*Mediterranean*

*Sea*

*SANJAK*
*NABLUS*

Jaffa
Nablus

Amman

*WILAYAT OF DAMASCUS*

Jerusalem

Gaza

Hebron

*SANJAK*
*KERAK*

Rafa

Kerak

El Arish

*WILAYAT OF*

Boundary Prior to 1906

*SANJAK JERUSALEM*

Armistice Separating Line 1906-1949

Sir Evelyn Barings (Lord Cromer) Decree (1892)

Administrative Armistice Line 1949-1967

Ma'an

Turkish Compromise Proposal

*DESERT*

*SINAI*
*WILAYAT OF*

Aqaba

Taba

*HEJAZ*

*Gulf of Suez*

*Gulf of Aqaba*

EGYPT

Ras Mohammed

*Red Sea*

25    50

km

MAJOR JEWISH CENTRE

CARTA Jerusalem

# 1919
# PARIS PROPOSALS BY THE ZIONIST MOVEMENT

★ At the beginning of the nineteenth century the Land was deserted and desolate. Its total population scarcely exceeded a quarter of a million. A Jewish community still clung to the Land. By the middle of the century Jews became the majority of the population in Jerusalem.

★ With the advent of modern nationalism and the increase of anti-semitism and anti-Jewish persecution the Zionist movement was founded at the turn of the century, following earlier attempts to establish new forms of agricultural villages based on equality and collectivism.

★ The goal of the Zionist movement, the re-establishment of a Jewish national home and State, was endorsed by many countries. It called for cooperation with the Arab national movement. The spokesman of that movement at the end of World War I, subsequently to become King Feisal of Iraq, signed an agreement with Chaim Weizmann, later to become Israel's first President, establishing a framework for cooperation between the projected Arab and Jewish States.

★ In 1919 the Zionist Movement submitted to the Paris Peace Conference proposals dealing with the reapportionment of the former Ottoman Empire. The proposals were termed "moderate and proper" by Feisal.

★ The map shows the boundaries suggested in those proposals.

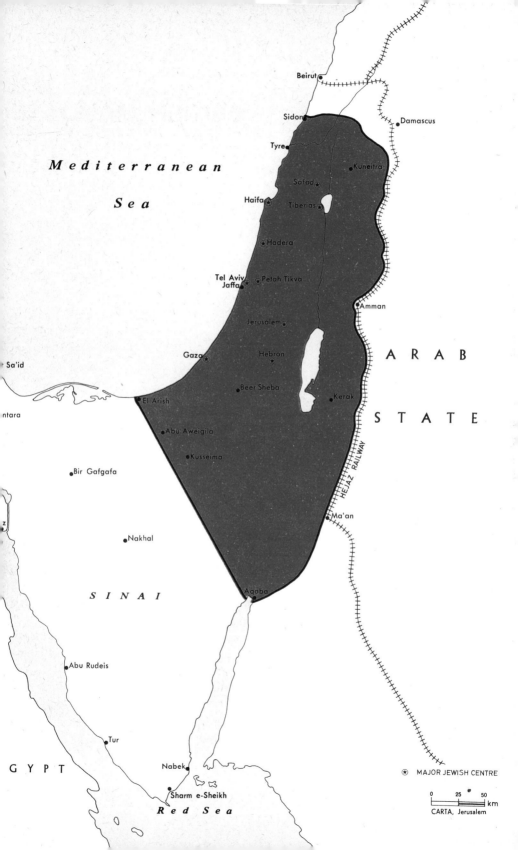

Beirut

Sidon

Tyre

Damascus

Kuneitra

Safad

Haifa

Tiberias

*Mediterranean*

*Sea*

Hadera

Tel Aviv
Jaffa

Petah Tikva

Amman

Jerusalem

**A R A B**

Gaza

Hebron

Sa'id

Beer Sheba

Kerak

**S T A T E**

El Arish

ntara

Abu Aweigila

Kusseima

Bir Gafgafa

HEJAZ RAILWAY

Ma'an

Nakhal

z

*S I N A I*

Aqaba

Abu Rudeis

Tur

Nabek

**G Y P T**

Sharm e-Sheikh

*Red Sea*

⊛ MAJOR JEWISH CENTRE

0    25    50
km

CARTA, Jerusalem

# BRITISH MANDATE

★   The boundaries of the Mandate over Palestine granted by the League of Nations on the British Government's express undertaking to carry out the Balfour Declaration calling for the establishment of the Jewish national home and specifically endorsing the Jewish people's attachment to the Land, were very different.

★   In the north, a major part of the Land, including the important Litani river, was detached and transferred to the Lebanon, primarily to satisfy French imperial ambitions. In the south, as a sop to Egypt's resentment of continued British occupation, it was decided to leave the border where it had been arbitrarily established in 1906.

★   On the other hand, in the east there was the compensatory award to the Arabs of much of the area between the Jordan river and Hejaz railway and present-day Iraq. What had been detached in the north and south had to be balanced by what was added in the east.

★   In the entire area, the British undertook to promote conditions leading to the establishment of the Jewish national home.

★   The map shows the area of the British Mandate as originally awarded by the League of Nations.

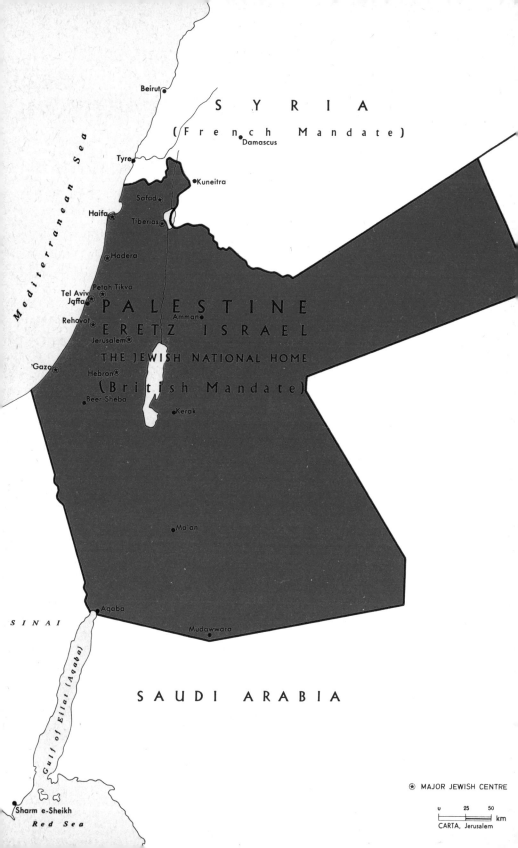

SYRIA

(French Mandate)

Beirut

Damascus

Tyre

Kuneitra

Safad

Haifa

Tiberias

Hadera

Petah Tikva

Tel Aviv

Jaffa

Rehovot

Jerusalem

Gaza

Hebron

Beer Sheba

Kerak

PALESTINE

ERETZ ISRAEL

THE JEWISH NATIONAL HOME

(British Mandate)

Amman

Ma'an

Mediterranean Sea

SINAI

Aqaba

Mudawwara

SAUDI ARABIA

Gulf of Eilat (Aqaba)

Sharm e-Sheikh

Red Sea

⊛ MAJOR JEWISH CENTRE

0    25    50

km

CARTA, Jerusalem

# 1922
# PARTITION

\* One year after the Mandate came into effect, Britain, in the fashion of previous imperial powers, divided the territory into two separate entities. The Emir Abdullah, one of the desert chieftains who had helped the British during World War I, had remained without a country as a result on Ibn Saud's seizure of the original kingdom of his father, the Sharif Hussein.

To provide him with a country of his own, and perhaps also to accede to Arab demands that the area of the Jewish national home be further limited, its entire eastern part, between the Jordan river and the Iraqi desert, was torn off to make the Emirate of Transjordan, with its capital in Amman.

\* No less than 91,000 square kilometres of the Land were thus cut off from it, including over 17,000 square kilometres of historic Palestine proper. The Peace Conference award had turned over 10,000 square kilometres of the historic Holy Land to Syria, 1,000 to the Lebanon and 3,000 to Egypt, leaving only a little over twenty thousand square kilometres between the Mediterranean and the Jordan river for future Jewish independence.

\* In that narrow area, rural and urban development proceeded rapidly, with scores of thousands of Jewish pioneers returning to their Homeland. The increasing prosperity and growing economic progress of the country attracted a great number of non-Jewish newcomers as well, and hundreds of thousands of Arabs streamed into the Land from the economically stagnant Arab countries around it.

\* The map shows the borders of the British mandated territory of Palestine between 1922 and 1948.

24

Beirut

S Y R I A
(F r e n c h   M a n d a t e)
Damascus

Tyre
Kuneitra

Safad
Haifa
Tiberias

Hadera
Netanya

Tel Aviv
Jaffa
Petah Tikva
Rehovot

Jerusalem

Gaza
Hebron

Beer Sheba

Amman

T R A N S   J O R D A N

(B r i t i s h   M a n d a t e)

Kerak

Ma'an

Mediterranean Sea

P A L E S T I N E
T H E   J E W I S H   N A T I O N A L   H O M E

S I N A I

Aqaba
Mudawwara

S A U D I   A R A B I A

Gulf of Eilat (Aqaba)

harm e-Sheikh

Red Sea

⊛ MAJOR JEWISH CENTRE

0     25     50
km

CARTA, Jerusalem

# 1947
# YET ANOTHER PARTITION

★    Even before outbreak of World War II Britain closed the gates of Palestine against Jewish immigration in appeasement of Arab terrorism and extremism (which had been fanned by Nazi support). Even when faced with the tragedy of European Jewry, Britain refused to rescind the restrictive measures enforced in violation of the spirit of the Mandate from the League of Nations and in spite of censure by the League's Permanent Mandates Commission.

★    After the Nazi holocaust in Europe and the plight of the Jewish refugees, pressure rose for absorption of Jews in their land.

★    Ultimately, Britain decided to transfer the problem to the United Nations. On 29 November, 1947, the General Assembly decided, with substantially more than the required two-thirds majority, to partition the Land once more into three parts, to be connected together in an economic union.

★    As shown in the map on the opposite page, there was to be a Jewish State and an Arab State, with the Jerusalem area a **corpus separatum.**

The plan would have cut the area of sovereign Israel still further to only 14,400 square kilometres. Yet in the interest of peace, and to provide an instant haven for Jewish refugees who could endure no longer in their camps overseas, the Jewish community accepted the proposal.

Instead of peace, the UN Resolution was followed by an outbreak of violence by Arab groups, aided and abetted by the neighbouring Arab countries. The Arabs were determined to prevent the establishment of any Jewish State, whatever its borders. Instead of peace and economic union, there followed war and sieges. Israel lost six thousand of its sons and daughters in its War of Independence.

Beirut

LEBANON

SYRIA

Damascus

Tyre

Kuneitra

Safad

Mediterranean

Haifa
Tiberias

Sea

Afula

Hadera

Netanya

Petah Tikva
Tel Aviv
Jaffa

Amman

Rehovot

Jerusalem

Gaza

Hebron

Sa'id

Beer Sheba

El Arish

Kerak

T
R
A
N
S
J
O
R
D
A
N

Ma'an

S I N A I

Aqaba

Mudawwara

Abu Rudeis

SAUDI ARABIA

G Y P T

⊛  MAJOR
   JEWISH CENTRE

   JEWISH STATE

   ARAB STATE

   INTERNATIONAL
   ZONE

0    25    50
              km
CARTA, Jerusalem

Sharm e-Sheikh

Red Sea

# 1949
# ARMISTICE AGREEMENTS

★　By the time the British Mandate ended on 15 May 1948 nothing was left of the partition plan. What is significant in the light of subsequent propaganda is that the proposed independent Arab State was never set up. Instead, Transjordan troops crossed the Jordan river and occupied most of what should have become that separate Arab State, destroying the Jewish villages which they found in their way. They laid siege to the Old City of Jerusalem, expelling its Jewish population and desecrating and razing to the ground all its ancient synagogues. Egypt overran the Gaza Strip.

★　The United Nations failed to intervene to uphold its own Resolution. The war came to an end only when it became clear, at the beginning of 1949, that the Arab States could not succeed in wiping out Israel's existence.

★　A series of separate armistice agreements were signed, all of which made it clear that the armistice lines established under them only reflected the military situation at the time. Thus, the Egyptian agreement (Article V, 2): states that "The armistice demarcation line is not to be construed in any sense as a political or territorial boundary and is delineated without prejudice as to rights, claims and positions of either party . . . "

Transjordan, which had changed its name to the Kingdom of Jordan, unilaterally in 1950 annexed the territory occupied by it in a measure recognized only by Britain and Pakistan. Israel immediately announced that she was reserving her rights regarding this territorial development. Egypt established a military administration in the Gaza Strip.

Notwithstanding Israel's admission to membership of the United Nations in May 1949, the Arab States persisted in their belligerency, continuing to declare their avowed aim of "throwing Israel into the sea." They refused to negotiate a final settlement.

★　The map shows the armistice lines provided for in the 1949 agreements.

**Jerusalem** (inset map)

(Jewish)

ISRAEL

Demilitarized Zone

Old City

(Arab)

No-man's Land

Demilitarized Zone

Armistice Line 1949

JORDAN

Beirut

LEBANON

Damascus

SYRIA

Tyre

Kuneitra

Nahariya

Safad

Akko

Haifa

Tiberias

Afula

Beit Shean

Hadera

Netanya

ISRAEL

Petah Tikva

Tel Aviv-

Jaffa

Amman

Rehovot

JORDAN

Jerusalem

Gaza

Hebron

Beer Sheba

Kerak

El Arish

Ma'an

SINAI

Eilat

Aqaba

Mudawwara

Gulf of Eilat (Aqaba)

SAUDI ARABIA

Abu Rudeis

Gulf of Suez

Dahab

EGYPT

Sharm e-Sheikh

Red Sea

| 0 | 25 | 50 |
|---|----|----|

km

CARTA, Jerusalem

# 1967
# CEASE – FIRE LINES

★   The Arab States did not confine their opposition to Israel's existence merely to verbal declarations. Contrary to an express Security Council Resolution they claimed the continued existence of a "state of war" between them and Israel. Using that claim, Egypt closed the Suez Canal and the Gulf of Aqaba to Israeli shipping.

In the early 'fifties, the Arabs began large-scale support of paramilitary terrorist operations against Israelis. In the summer of 1956, Egypt concluded a military alliance with the Arab states bordering Israel, bringing their armies under her command, and launched a massive offensive military buildup in Sinai.

★   In exercise of its right of self-defence Israel struck back in 1956 and its forces reached the Suez Canal, breaking the blockade of the Straits of Tiran. The other Arab States refused to follow Egypt's lead and at that time stayed out of the battle.

★   The United States and the Soviet Union together exerted pressure on Israel to withdraw even without a final peace settlement. The maritime Powers guaranteed freedom of passage in the Gulf, and the Canal, too, was to be open to Israeli shipping. A UN force was set up to patrol the Gaza Strip, Sinai and the entrance to the Gulf, and the Powers undertook to see that serious efforts were made towards final and permanent peace. Nothing came of any of this.

★   In 1967, threatening once more to destroy Israel, Egypt massed hundreds of tanks, guns and planes in the Sinai desert, summarily expelled the UN force and reimposed a blockade in the Gulf. All the intricate network of international arrangements and guarantees disappeared overnight, and Israel was once more left on its own. The result was the Six Day War.

Jordan, in spite of an express appeal by Israel, refused to stay out of the war, and opened an artillery barrage on Jerusalem's New City. Syria came in as well.

★   The map shows the 1967 cease-fire lines.

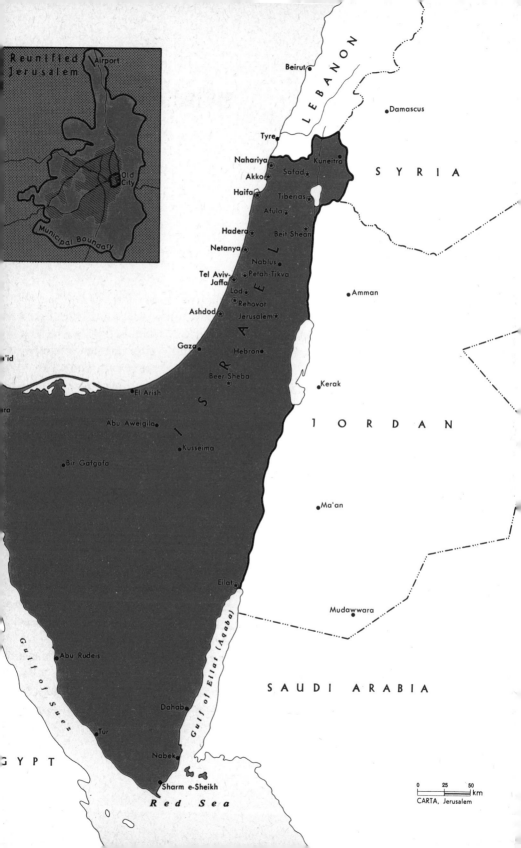

Reunified
Jerusalem

Airport

Old
City

Municipal Boundary

Beirut

Damascus

LEBANON

SYRIA

Tyre

Nahariya

Akko

Haifa

Safad

Kuneitra

Tiberias

Afula

Beit Shean

Hadera

Netanya

Nablus

Tel Aviv-
Jaffa

Petah-Tikva

Lod

Rehovot

Ashdod

Jerusalem

Gaza

Hebron

Beer Sheba

El Arish

Abu Aweigila

Kusseima

Bir Gafgafa

I S R A E L

Amman

Kerak

J O R D A N

Ma'an

Mudawwara

Eilat

Abu Rudeis

Gulf of Eilat (Aqaba)

SAUDI ARABIA

Dahab

Gulf of Suez

Tur

GYPT

Nabek

Sharm e-Sheikh

Red Sea

0   25   50
km

CARTA, Jerusalem

# BORDER SEESAW

★ Ever since the end of the fighting of June 1967, Israel has been appealing to the Arab States to meet with it and discuss a final peace settlement and sign peace treaties. On 22 November 1967 the Security Council called for "just and lasting peace", after all the attempts of the Arabs and their allies to push through a resolution calling for the reestablishment of the status quo ante had proved abortive.

★ As provided for in the Security Council Resolution, Israel declared its readiness to exchange the cease-fire lines for "secure and agreed boundaries". While bearing in mind its historic rights and national attachment to the patrimony of the Jewish people, Israel has made it clear that it seeks not arbitrary annexation but borders related primarily to security needs.

★ The Arabs have attained independence in fourteen sovereign States, comprising an area of some ten million square kilometres. Israel's only desire in its own small historic Homeland is to coexist with the Arab States in a system of regional friendship and cooperation. It has never sought to interfere in the internal regimes of the Arab States. It is for the Palestinian Arabs, who make up eighty percent of the population of the Kingdom of Jordan, to decide how they wish to express their national aspirations in the territories between Israel's eastern border and the Iraqi frontier.

★ Israel will not agree nor can it be expected to agree to a re-division of Jerusalem. Nor can Israel permit the return of hostile military concentrations to within range of its cities and within minutes' flying distance of its major centres of population. There must be open frontiers and peaceful cooperation for the benefit of the region as a whole.

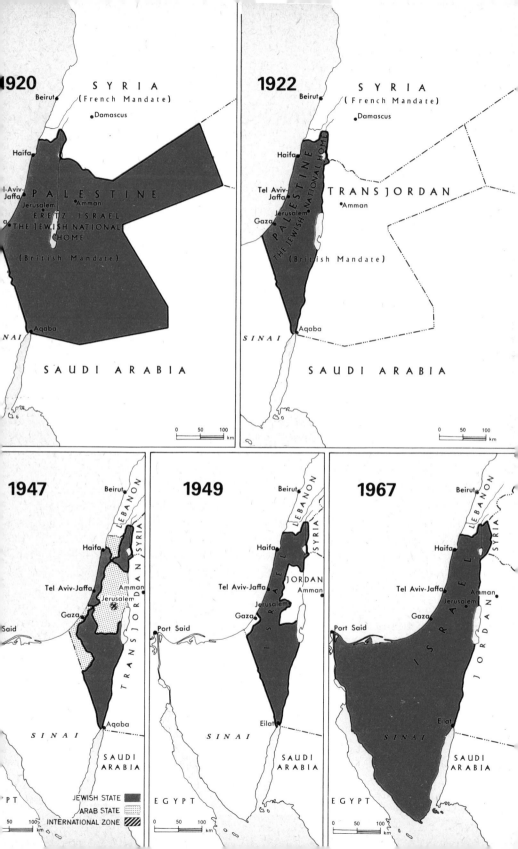

# CREATING SECURE BORDERS

★ Until June 1967, the Egyptian army had been stationed within ten minutes' walking distance from Israeli villages; today, they are 400 kilometres away. The Jordanian army previously had been 15 km. from Tel Aviv and was actually inside Jerusalem. Its guns at Kalkiliya shelled Tel Aviv in June 1967. Today they are 90 km. from Tel Aviv, and 40 km. from Jerusalem.

Before June 1967, an enemy offensive would have found Israel fighting in her main centres of population. Today, such an enemy offensive would not directly threaten her urban centres.

In addition, the present distance of the nearest Egyptian air force bases from Israel's major centres of population adds an essential security dimension.

This dimension is vitally important to Israel since the Soviet Union has provided the UAR with ground-to-air and ground-to-ground missiles. The military presence of Soviet forces in the UAR also imposes upon Israel special considerations in determining the geographical dimensions of its security.

★ Following the Six-Day War Israel's land borders have been considerably shortened. The border with Egypt was 265 km. long and is now only 160 km.; that with Jordan has been shortened from about 561 km. to 300 km. This has made the frontiers far more defensible than before.

★ Israel maintains that the final "secure and recognized boundaries" should be identical neither with the armistice lines of 1949 nor with the cease-fire lines of 1967. The determination of such boundaries thus awaits negotiation between the two sides.

Israel adhered to the Security Council Resolution to cease fire. The cease-fire lines established at the time are still in force, pending a peace treaty. The Security Council rejected the Soviet proposal to call for Israel's withdrawal from the cease-fire lines.

# THE VULNERABLE
# ARMISTICE LINES
# 1949 – 1967

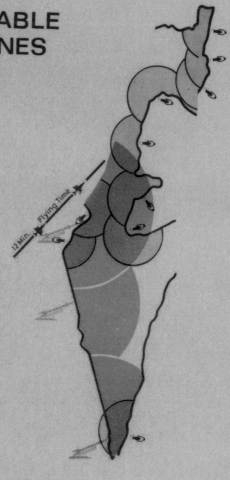

MISSILE RANGE

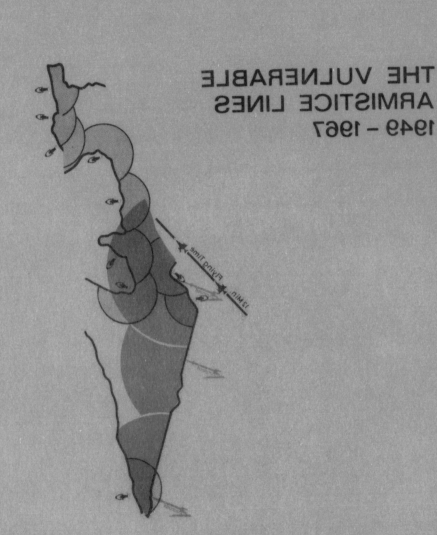

# FRONTIER CHANGES IN EUROPE

In calling for the establishment of final, agreed, secure and recognized borders, Israel only follows the established practice following
wars. The following maps show frontier changes in Europe at the end
of World Wars I and II, the outcome of peaceful negotiations.

The changes conform with standard precedents even in the case
of existing political borders, and should especially hold true for Israel,
whose final borders are yet to be determined.

The Soviet Union has been in the forefront of those calling for
unconditional return to the status quo ante in the Middle East in plain
departure from its own practice in Eastern Europe. There is truth in a
commentary in "Pravda" of 2 September 1964:

**"The borders of the State have become sanctified in the efforts of the
settlers in the border villages and by the streams of blood which they
have had to shed in their defence. A people which has been attacked
and which defended itself and emerged victorious has the sacred right
of establishing for itself such a final political settlement as would permit
it to liquidate the sources of aggression ... a people which has acquir-
ed its security with such heavy sacrifice will never agree to restore
the old borders".**

It is a truth that should be applied in the case of Israel, too.

# EUROPE

Following both World Wars,
extensive frontier changes were made throughout Europe,
**through peaceful negotiations.**
This map shows the extent of these changes.

38

# U.S.S.R.

**Article III, Soviet–Federal German Republic Treaty of 1970:**
"In accordance with the aforementioned aims and principles, the Federal Republic of Germany and the Union of Soviet Socialist Republics are agreed on the recognition that peace in Europe can only be maintained when no one infringes the present frontiers.

"They oblige themselves to respect unreservedly the territorial integrity of all States in Europe in their present frontiers.

"They declare that they have no territorial demands against anyone, nor will they have such in the future.

"They regard the frontiers of all the States in Europe today and in future as inviolable, as they stand on the day of the signing of this treaty, including the Oder-Neisse line . . ."

[The New York Times, August 12, 1970]

Switzerland (drawn on the same scale), on this and the following pages, provides a standard of comparison which enables us to appreciate the extent of territorial changes.

# FEDERAL REPUBLIC OF GERMANY AND POLAND

**Article I(1) of the Federal Republic of Germany–Polish Treaty of 1970:**
"The Federal Republic of Germany and the People's Republic of Poland
state in mutual agreement that the existing boundary line, the course
of which is laid down in Charter IX of the decisions of the Potsdam
Conference of August 2, 1945, as running from the Baltic Sea immediately west of Swinemuende, thence along the Oder River to the
confluence of the Western Neisse River and along the Western Neisse
to the Czechoslovak frontier, shall constitute the Western State
frontier of the People's Republic of Poland."

[International Herald Tribune, November 21–22, 1970]

# RUMANIA

**The terms of the Rumanian armistice with the Allies, Article 2:**
"The frontier established by the Soviet–Rumanian Agreement of June 28, 1940, is restored."

> [As announced by Radio Moscow,
> 13 September 1944, Keesing p. 6690]

# CZECHOSLOVAKIA

**Czechoslovak–USSR Treaty, 29 June 1945:**
"The Transcarpathian Ukraine, according to the Czechoslovak Consti-
tution called Subcarpathian Russia, which on the basis of the Treaty
of St Germain-en-Laye of September 10, 1919, became an autonomous
unit within the Czechoslovak Republic, is reunited, in accordance with
the desire of its inhabitants, and on the basis of friendly agreement
between the contracting Parties, with its ancient mother country, the
Ukraine, and incorporated in the Ukrainian Soviet Republic."

# FINLAND

**Peace Treaty between USSR and Finland, 1940, Article 9:**
"The new State frontiers have been fixed on a new line according to
which the following territories are included in Soviet Russia:
"The whole of the Karelian Isthmus, with the City of Viipuri ... "

**Peace Treaty with Finland, 1947, Article 2:**
"In accordance with the Armistice Agreement of September 19, 1944,
Finland confirms the return to the Soviet Union of the province of
Petsamo (Pechenga) ... "
Article 4:
"Finland shall lease the peninsula of Hankö to Soviet Russia for a
period of 30 years, with all islands situated in this area ... Finland
agrees to the establishment there of a Soviet military base for pro-
tective purposes ... "

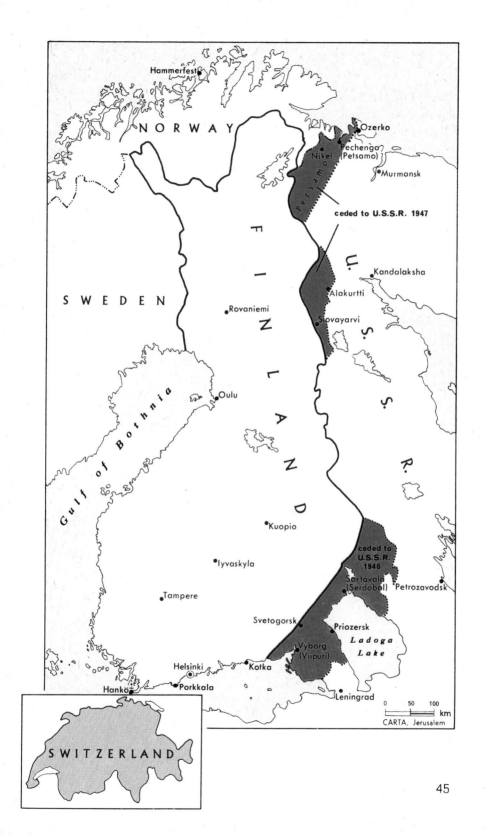

Hammerfest

NORWAY

Ozerko
Pechenga
Nikel (Petsamo)
Murmansk

ceded to U.S.S.R. 1947

SWEDEN

Kandalaksha

Rovaniemi

Alakurtti

Siovayarvi

Oulu

Gulf of Bothnia

FINLAND

U.S.S.R.

Kuopio

ceded to
U.S.S.R.
1940

Iyvaskyla

Sortavala
(Serdobol)
Petrozavodsk

Tampere

Svetogorsk

Priozersk

Ladoga
Lake

Vyborg
(Viipuri)

Helsinki
Hanko
Porkkala
Kotka
Leningrad

0    50    100
km

CARTA, Jerusalem

SWITZERLAND

45

# ITALY

**Article 3(i) of Treaty of Peace with Italy, 1947:**
"The new frontier follows a line starting from the junction of the frontiers of Austria, Italy and Yugoslavia as they existed on January 1, 1938, and proceeding southward along the 1938 frontier between Yugoslavia and Italy to the junction of that frontier with the administrative boundary between the Italian provinces of Frindi (Udine) and Gorizia..."

**Memorandum of Understanding between the Governments of Italy, the UK, the USA and Yugoslavia, 1954:**
"As soon as this Memorandum of Understanding has been initialled and the boundary adjustments provided by it have been carried out..."

# FRANCE

# BELGIUM

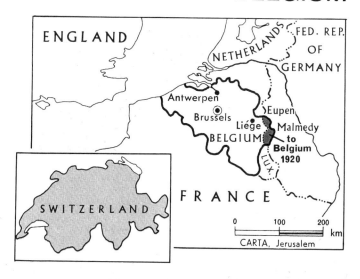

# GREECE

# DENMARK